SOUL WEALTH

Finding Vision, Compassion, Authenticity,
Abundance and Legacy in The Midst of Chaos

Dr. Vikki Johnson

Pecan Tree Publishing,
Hollywood, Fl

Soul Wealth: Finding Vision, Compassion, Authenticity, Abundance
and Legacy In The Midst Of Chaos

Dr. Vikki Johnson

ISBN: 978-1-7328311-9-3 (Paperback)
Library of Congress Control Number: 2019905750

Cover design by: Dimitrinka Cvetkoski
Interior Design by: Rodolfo Samson
Front and back Author Cover Photo: Cheriss May for http://www.cherissmay.com

Printed in the United States of America
First printing edition 2019
Pecan Tree Publishing
Hollywood, FL 33020

PECAN TREE PUBLISHING

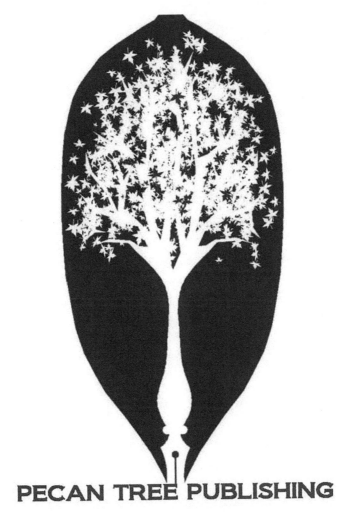

PECAN TREE PUBLISHING

WWW.PECANTREEBOOKS.COM

INFO@PECANTREEBOOKS.COM

PRAISE AND APPLAUSE FOR THE WORK OF SOUL WEALTH

"Step out of chaos and into your SOUL WEALTH! Crisis is a part of life, yet chaos is optional. Dr. Vikki is living proof that there is a powerful alternative to suffering in the chaos…choosing to shape-shift it! Often, our perceptions of the crises we experience leave us paralyzed in a state of chaos. Chaos is a place of disorder and confusion that can bankrupt the soul, causing one to deplete internal resources, exhaust external options and operate in perpetual dysfunction (living beneath Divine birthright). In this empowering and transparent road map, Dr. Vikki guides the reader on a journey from hurt to healing by providing insight that helps one to find meaning and resilience in the face of conflict that life presents."

Rev. Anika Wilson Brown, MSW, LGSW
www.anikawilsonbrown.com

"Soul Wealth is boldly prioritizing, practicing and passionately celebrating your most intrinsic needs and desires to experience optimum abundance - mind, body and spirit."
Veronica Very, CEO/Founder
Wonder of Women International
www.thewonderofwomen.org

In SOUL WEALTH: Finding Vision, Compassion, Authenticity, Abundance and Legacy in The Midst of Chaos, author Vikki Johnson has created a revolution of the mind, body and spirit that will take her readers on a journey that should be experienced by everyone. The journey of understanding how to tap into the essence of one's being to live a more authentic and fulfilled life, which is a true gift. Vikki Johnson's gift gives you the blueprint for unleashing and walking in wealth...SOUL WEALTH!

Sonia Jackson Myles, CEO and Chief Dreamwalker
The Accord Group LLC

"People hear the word wealth and automatically think of money. Soul Wealth encompasses so much more. Soul Wealth exudes the essence of abundance and wholeness in every area of life.In a world bankrupt of spiritual wholeness, we could all use more Soul Wealth."

Jeri A. Dyson, MD
Physician, Author, Global Speaker, Intimacy Expert
Founder, Global Girls Global Women, Inc.
www.globalgirlsglobalwomen.org

South Wealth means spiritual fulfillment. It means peace in being who I am as I am. It means that I am doing what God has called me to do in a way that brings me spiritual abundance! It is the highest form of richness.Vikki is the epitome of sisterhood. She moves through the world sharing love, instilling faith, encouraging connection while challenging women to live in a way that honors their very soul! Her heart is an endless well from which to draw hope - hope in yourself, hope in God and hope in others! Her words of wisdom nourish your heart and stimulates your mind. Her presence shifts the environment and inspires women to experience the wealth of their own SOULS...SOUL WEALTH!

SharRon Jamison

www.SharRonJamison.com

Four words: She. Changed. My. Life! From our very first meeting Dr. Vikki Johnson has lovingly, compassionately, and tenderly planted seeds in my life that a decade later are still bearing fruit.

Wendi Cherry, Visionary

The Goddess Awakening and Healing Sanctuary

goddess-awaken.com

"They say there's a glass sea in heaven, where you can see your reflection in the water. In this picture of yourself you are whole, happy, healed, and at peace. In her book "Soul Wealth: Finding Vision, Compassion, Authenticity, Abundance and Legacy in The Midst of Chaos", Dr. Vikki Johnson is like that piece of heaven. Get ready to be free from all of the things that rob you of your true joy."

Veda McCoy, Founder

Unlock Your Life and Unlocked Women's Collective

PREFACE

Thank you, Vikki, for creating "Soul Wealth" and abundance for me in this moment!

When Vikki asked me to write the Preface for this book, I felt an elevated state of gratitude. Dr. Vikki Johnson fills my heart with love and the incredible gift of Spirit she brings to my space on this planet.

Applaud yourself for being drawn to the energy of this book. You've made a great first step toward enriching your soul. Now you are on the journey to spiritual, mental, emotional, relational and financial wealth. Vikki has created a brilliant, resourceful platform to manifest wealth from the soul level – even during life's chaotic interruptions.

I first met Vikki as my college roommate at Howard University in Washington, D.C. We gave one another a compliment in the hallway of the freshman dorm. That was the beginning of a lifelong spirit-to-spirit connection of sisterhood built on unconditional love, acceptance, tolerance, respect and loyalty. Vikki has always been, at least in my mind, 'A GIVER' to this planet.

I can recall at her 40th birthday celebration; Vikki made it a party for all her guests born in December. Each of us was pampered throughout her celebration; each of us honored, remembered and anointed with positive affirmations and gifts. The memory of this gesture has stayed with me. It is emblematic of Vikki's ability to create abundance in the space where scarcity occupies. She spoke to me with that gesture – our souls are abundantly wealthy – if we only are open to its possibilities. From that day forward, I learned to live in the space of abundance and no longer scarcity. I became like Vikki - the wealthiest woman on this planet. It is from this experience that I am honored to wholeheartedly recommend this book.

Think about it…all the answers you look for so diligently from others, situations, experiences, always begin with a thought. And guess what? You will see and hear the answers that were always deep within your authentic self. Vikki's experiences will be familiar to all readers on this life's journey, reinforcing the legitimacy of her messages.

You will experience a tremendous shift in your total way of being while reading Vikki's book. You get to restate: …who am I? What am I committed to inventing, creating and discovering with myself or in myself using the tools, inspirations, and lessons I will learn and be open to from this powerful read?

Vikki's book recalls the words from a Bliss song: "Jump off that cliff and be who you were born to be!" You're listening now to your inner observer who is only capable of the truth - your truth about who you were created to be in this world. You get to co-author it with your source of higher understanding and consciousness along with help from your higher power, guides and teachers.

This book recalls a classic story and one of my favorites: The Wizard of Oz. We are all on that "Yellow Brick Road" traveling through life.

Who will be crossing your path? Who will be your Lion, Scarecrow, Tin Man?

For me, the important character is Toto – the one that pulled open the curtain on the Wizard – so we could see the unknown possibilities of coming from a space where nothing exists. Only after we discover (with God's help) that no one has power over us but us can we build a foundation of certainty.

Vikki is a powerful, soulful, beautiful, abundant, giving creative leader. You have chosen her to assist you on your yellow brick road journey to freedom. This book has been birthed to give hope. It is about transforming a future once thought to be restricted and closed into one that is unlimited. This book is about confronting and converting the happenings of your life into moments of growth that allow you to live your greatest, most elevated life.

Blessings, Peace and Light from my soul to yours!

Tori D. Hodge, MSW, RLCSWI, and Ontological Life Coach

FOREWORD

I can't write enough words to convey the way I feel about Vikki Johnson. She truly has changed my life. She was recommended as a speaker for my IAMAWARRIOR TOUR in 2015. The moment I met her she touched my heart. She not only greeted me with open arms, but she touched my soul. Vikki has a glow about her that many women don't exude. She has the essence of an angel because she is so giving, loving and most of all uplifting. When she shared with a room of 250 women at that conference, she was so open and raw about her life. I knew she and I would be connected for years. I felt the same way when I was going through Stage 4 breast cancer and a horrible divorce. I connected with her on the shame, suffering, embarrassment and more.

I knew Vikki Johnson, a woman who could come on my stage, strip herself down to being so raw and tell her truth was someone I could connect with forever. She has been a friend, confidante and an uplifting soul sister. There are few women who truly help and look out for other women. Fewer are those who will take time out of their day to really help you with advice, support or just a shoulder to cry on. Rare are the women who truly give you the shirt off their back and help you join forces with someone else; and who go above and beyond for you or anyone you know simply because you asked. I must say that woman who goes overboard for you, who fights for you and who cheers you on to win is Vikki Johnson. She truly is like no other woman I know.

Bershan Shaw,
TV Personality, Warrior Life Coach; International Motivational
Speaker and Author
www.urawarrior.com
www.bershanshaw.com
Follow: Twitter @bershanshaw and Instagram @bershanshaw

INTRODUCTION

Life happens to us all. While not the desired result, it is easy to get stuck in the difficult places as they unfold. Settling in the paradigm of struggle or the cave of self-doubt or the prism of pain requires very little effort. It is a default response. Frequently hard places harden hearts and close minds to the joy of possibility. The result is a life of anger, sabotage, illness, deep disappointment, toxic relationships, unhealthy behaviors, sadness, poverty, superficiality and pretentiousness.

Too many people have simply given up on their hopes and dreams. Some have embraced mediocrity as being their best while others have succumbed to frustration, discouragement, pessimism and hopelessness as their unchangeable reality. In this place the routine is to sit back and covet the success of others while secretly and consistently replaying every failure, traumatic event or missed opportunity they have experienced.

My intention in this book is to take you on a journey of self-awareness. Read with the expectation that you will become unapologetic about who you are, what you desire and how you are to "show up fully" in this world. My desire is for you to have such CLARITY that by the time you finish reading you are awakened to the best days of your life. You are inspired to live NOW.

Through my own experiences of trepidation, shame, loneliness and fear, I share my life lessons in these pages. With transparency and love I offer you the wisdom I have gained in my own process of healing! I desperately needed relief from the residue of sadness, betrayal, post-partum depression, bad choices, abandonment, bankruptcy, abortion, miscarriage, foreclosure, car repossession, infidelity, getting laid off a job I loved, feeling forgotten, overlooked and so much more. That was my world of chaos inside a world (or our world) where we are bombarded with chaos daily.

How did I find the peace that surpasses all understanding that softened my heart and opened my mind to the probability that I could live an ascended life? The answer is I genuinely got sick and tired of mismanaging my life, protecting an image that was killing me, dressing it up on the outside while inspiring, encouraging and uplifting others. Meanwhile I was absolutely broken, miserable and truly unhappy with my life as it was at that time. Some days I just felt helpless and hopeless. My heart was sick. There just had to be more. One day in a moment of stillness God whispered, "There is SO much more Vikki." I believe with all my heart that was the day I got pregnant with SOUL WEALTH, which is vision, compassion, authenticity, abundance and legacy. Soul Wealth is not about money or the accumulation of assets. Soul Wealth is cultivated internally with external payoffs. Once you get it and implement it in your daily experience then your life will never be the same.

TABLE OF CONTENTS

SOUL WEALTH MANIFESTO

WRITTEN BY SANJO JENDAYI

AUTHENTIC

I descend into the depths of my soul to find my AUTHENTIC SELF. I speak and live my truth without forcing it onto others. I honor myself and others. Nothing outside of my true, real and genuine substance can define me. I AM walking in my AUTHENTIC BEINGNESS.

COMPASSION

I nurture, heal and uplift my INNER-me which fuels my compassion for self and others. I sit quietly as I ascend to hear my Higher Self. I empathize with others without sacrificing self. Grace and Mercy walk with me. I AM love therefore I AM loving and lovable.

ABUNDANCE

I recognize that abundance is all encompassing and does not begin nor end with material gain. I am also aware of the differences between clutter and abundance thereby letting go of that which depletes my soul. I attract abundance. I AM RICH! I AM thankful for intangible prosperity such as good health, a sane mind, loving friends and family.

I live a soul directed life carrying out my soul's purpose increasing my SOUL WEALTH daily!

I AM WEALTHY!

VISION

"Write the vision and make it plain so they that read it can run with it.
Though it is delayed wait for it. It's coming for sure."
Habakkuk 2:2-3

"Where there is no vision you will be destroyed."
Proverbs 29:18

I am sure you have heard of snow angels. Growing up in South Florida we didn't have snow, so as a little girl I used to make grass angels. I would lay in my front yard for what seemed like hours staring at the sky and daydreaming. I honestly thought I was an alien and one day my ride back home would show up to take me above the clouds. Isn't that something? The high place was calling me even as a child.

Vision is born of chaos. Where there is chaos there is a lack of understanding. Vision is often the result of revolutionary actions. Without a vision you will be destroyed. As I write this book it seems as if the world is filled with people without vision. Chaos is everywhere. As I pen these words, 800-thousand federal employees are furloughed or not earning a paycheck because (in my opinion), the current President has no vision. You see, without vision there is a tendency to create as you go. The United States of America is in chaos - yet not without hope.

My desire and intention are to guide you to find vision, compassion, authenticity, abundance and legacy in the midst of chaos. Peace is possible in chaos. It is inner peace. Vision is possible, especially in chaos, because it is required to navigate uncertainty. Vision is about having a blueprint based on a dream. Take your dream and write it out. Now you have a road map to a better life and a better you. We receive what we see and prepare for in our lives. Activate your imagination now. Visualize the life you want now. See it. Say it. Believe it. Imagine it. Feel it. Manifest it.

I remember years ago I was in an exceptionally low place mentally, emotionally, spiritually and physically. I was recovering from a bad accident which required two surgeries, 12 weeks of absolute bed rest and an entire year of learning to walk again. I had little to no energy. All I wanted to do was sleep. I didn't want to talk to or be around people. I had lost my vision, my passion and my hope.

One day while at home thinking about nothing, God gave me an open vision. An open vision is like a vivid daydream you intuitively know is from God. In the vision I was on a big stage standing behind a podium with a microphone in my hand. I was speaking to a large crowd. Some people were crying, others laughing, some waving their hands, others smiling, some sitting and others standing. They were all responding to what I was saying with tremendous emotion. God said to me, "Vikki that is you!" I was a bit confused because at that time I was not a speaker nor had any desire to be a speaker. I was a young wife, recovering from a severe injury and was about to be or already depressed.

I heard God; yet dismissed what He said, but I never forgot the vision. Twenty-five years later I am living that exact vision and more. Whew! I know for a fact that God had to show me something at that time in my life because I was alive but not living. Thank God for the power of vision.

The purpose of vision is to push you, nudge you, empower you and encourage you to keep going. David Gikandi, Author of "A Happy Pocket Full of Money" said, "Life is images of the mind expressed." In other words, your life follows your thoughts and your words. David goes on to say, "visualize your wildest dreams and fantasies then back it up with faith, belief and certainty." I will add decisive action must accompany the aforementioned qualities, because faith without works means nothing. You really can have whatever you like. You must imagine or vision it first.

SOUL WEALTH AFFIRMATIONS FOR VISION

Started from the bottom now we're here! When you've been knocked down the ONLY alternative is to look up so you can be inspired, grow up so you can be trusted, and then go up to where you belong to make a difference in the world. Where you are is not all there is! Keep looking up!

Often before drinking something naturally good for us it is necessary to vigorously shake the bottle so what has SETTLED at the bottom can get back in the mix to activate all the nutrients. Loved ones; some of us have SETTLED at the bottom of our respective spheres of influ-ence because we've been dormant for too long. Consequently, and in this apostolic season, we must be vigorously **shaken awake** so that we can get back in the mix to activate and be who we are designed to be.

God whispered this to me, and I'm inspired to share with you because I really am excited about your future too! "The QUICKER you stop the old the SOONER you start the new!"

Another portal of manifestation has opened to those of us courageous enough to let go of what was.

COMPASSION

"God's loyalty and love never ends.
His compassion never stops.
It is new every morning.
Lord your loyalty and faithfulness is abundant."
Lamentations 3:22

Let the last time you betrayed yourself be the last time you betray yourself. Show yourself some compassion. Love yourself the way you love the people you say you love. Be gentle with yourself. Give yourself a break. Stop judging yourself and - by all means - set yourself free.

What I know for sure is the moment I stopped comparing myself to others is the moment guilt and the feeling of defeat left my life. The Bible says in Jeremiah 31:3 "With lovingkindness have I drawn you and continued my faithfulness to you." It follows if God is gentle with me, I should be gentle with me too.

Many times a day I talk to myself. I reassure myself with words of life, love and power. I hug myself. I affirm myself. I have had to minister to and encourage myself many days and nights. Compassion is for you first – then - others. We can't give away what we don't have.

Compassion has provoked me to release toxic relationships and embrace others that I felt unworthy of having in my life. Compassion will heal your broken soul and mend your broken heart. Compassion will comfort you when you are grieving and tend to you when you are not feeling well. Compassion is mandatory to live peaceably with yourself and others. Compassion is required to forgive yourself. Compassion is what you need to strive for better.

It was compassion that caused me to walk away from a verbally and emotionally abusive relationship. It was compassion that constrained me to take better care of my emotions and thought life. It was compassion that allowed me to start making decisions that honored me instead of violated my standards. Compassion is your friend. Treat her well. *(Yes, compassion is feminine says me)*

Compassion moved me to give my cousin one of my kidneys on June 17, 2010. It was one of the most transforming times of my life. What moved me more, however; was my family's and my surgeon's response to my decision. Here is an excerpt from an email sent to the family from his sister postsurgery:

> *"Three years ago, June 5, 2007, my sister sent out a "blast email" to you, our family. She told you how our brother needed a kidney and that he needed to start dialysis. Everyone showed deep concern and support. Everyone responded! On June 14, 2007, Vikki responded. She said, "I'm O+ too, maybe I'm the chosen one. I'll call him today."*

> *If you didn't know, Vikki was **the** match, **the** chosen one and she did it! On June 17, 2010, Vikki gave our brother a kidney, her kidney! What a sacrifice! The surgeries went well. I am so overwhelmed with all that has happened; the beauty and power of our family, especially Vikki! She's given my brother life again! Do you know how powerful that is?! I want the world to know how much I love her! She went into the hospital healthy and with no pain. She's in some discomfort now (putting it lightly). Please pray for her; hold her up, give her strength while she endures the discomfort and adjustment that her body is going through.*

> *As a little girl I remember my dad and Uncle always acknowledging each other by yelling "Blood". Instead of saying a name, what's going on or hey to that person - they'd*

yell out, "Blood!" No matter how much time had passed since they'd seen each other, they were ALWAYS ex-cited about getting together (I loved watching them)! One would yell "Blood!" and the other one would respond, "Blood!" Today I understand the significance of that more than ever!

I just want to say, Vikki is BEAUTIFUL! Our mom says Vikki is an ANGEL! The gift of life and a kidney is priceless! I love you Vikki! BLOOD! BLOOD!"

Whew! This still touches me. I have been in great health since. God is an awesome God and has obligated Himself to our well-being when we lead with, live from and love from a place of compassion. How great is our God! His compassion never ends - neither should ours.

SOUL WEALTH AFFIRMATIONS FOR COMPASSION

Even though I continue to declare, "Be not weary in well doing for in due season I shall reap if I don't faint;" I still thought I needed an intervention. Then God said, "You're not in crisis you're at a crossroad about to crossover into a place of perpetual abundance, peace and intangible prosperity. HOLD ON!" God is perfecting everything that concerns you.

FORGIVE. FORGIVE. FORGIVE. FORGIVE. FORGIVE. However, forgiveness doesn't mean you bypass common sense. Sometimes your "Seven Last Words" should be: "I forgive you, but we are done." It is okay for forgiveness to be the final frontier of a relationship. The ultimate understanding of forgiveness is trusting that the benefit of that lesson will be greater than the pain it caused. Whew!!!

There is so much more to your life than where you currently are. When my daughter was just a little girl it was an exceedingly challenging time for me. Post-partum depression is very real for many women. I was one of them. It took me years to feel like a Mom ready to handle the responsibility of motherhood. I'm so glad I was surrounded by people who cared for me when I couldn't really care for myself, let alone my child. I share this to encourage some mother, some woman to KEEP GOING even if it's just one moment, one breath at a time. The joy of what's coming will more than make up for the sadness, disappointments and struggle of your past and the struggle of your now.

If you have an anointing to heal others expect to attract a lot of broken, sick, dysfunctional people into your life. It's not about you, nor is their behavior personal toward you. It's an assignment!

People spend a lot of time in all types of relationships that don't nurture their soul. When people show you they are not interested in relating with you in the spirit of reciprocity confidently walk away. There are people who would be honored to be in your life, and they will consistently display the same. Go in peace not pieces!

I practice radical self-care because I am familiar with my body and know when I am out of balance. This practice came in part, because I concluded that I'd been holding onto a LOT of toxic emotions instead of addressing and saying some things to some people. While sitting in my favorite place, God whispered to my heart: "Vikki when you have those uncomfortable conversations it will increase your capacity to receive what you need for where you're going." I had to talk to quite a few people quickly. May the truth set you free or not; because I am no longer willing to carry what doesn't belong to me so others can be okay!

What's going on in your life right now is not forever! You have grace to pull yourself together. Gather the pieces that still work and keep it moving. WHAT YOU HAVE LEFT IS ENOUGH!

The timing of God is perfect! One thing I know for sure is that God won't leave you hopeless. During major transitions in my life I have had and do have PERFECT PEACE! God has been too faithful in my life for me to doubt now. When you know what you know and have proof from your past that it always works out…don't allow other people's panic to disrupt your peace!

When you can do good because it's in your capacity/power/authority to help somebody - DO IT! The "Golden Rule" (that I learned in kindergarten) says you should do so because the day WILL COME when you will need someone with the capacity/power/authority to do the same for you or someone you love.

The US Presidential election of 2016 exposed what has been simmering in this country all along. Racism is real. Chaos is real. What we know is that some people felt (and still feel) released to display their arrogance. What many are experiencing emotionally (especially people of color) is TRAUMA! People are tired, afraid and truth be told many feel hopeless. I provoke us to face these feelings, have uncomfortable conversations, and most importantly take corrective ACTION toward self-sufficiency particularly in economic freedom. We can no longer be passive while "waiting on God" to fix our failures as a community. Who are YOU called to BE in the earth that will effect sustainable change? God adds "super" to our natural which THEN gives us all sufficiency in Him. THIS IS A CALL TO ACTION!

We spend so much time, (too much time actually) trying to be in relationship with people who are not trying to be in relationship with us. Stop supporting people who don't support you! You can love and respect them without chasing them. Nurture those who fill you up, invest in you, are there for you, are called to be in your life and who make you a better person. As I grow older, I'm more at peace with the fact that quality is more valuable than quantity. If you're not sure about someone then ask yourself, "What have they done for me lately?" Especially ask this question if you're the one always giving. Know who is in your inner circle!

Be intentional about nurturing the proven relationships in your life. Stop giving time, energy, money, effort to people you are trying to impress into covenant. It is not sustainable. Be honest about who is toxic in your life then detox your connections. Be a good steward of the people who honor you, love you in actions not just words, pray for you and speak life to you. Once you do that consistently God will intersect your path with those divinely assigned to be in your life to elevate you to your next dimension.

Radical choices create radical changes which produce radical results. Do something that makes your life unrecognizable even to you!

There is a LOT going on in the world competing for our attention. Be still. Get quiet. REMEMBER TO BREATHE! Focus. Get your affairs in order. Get life insurance if you don't have any and make sure you have enough if you do have it. Tell people you love that you love them. Get adequate sleep. Guard your heart. Follow peace. Laugh a lot. Hug tightly. Pray without ceasing. Lead with love. Forgive quickly. Live your best life NOW!

Sometimes you just need to let things fall apart so God can put them back together with what you should have had in the first place.

LIFE IS SHORT!!! Stop wasting time AND money on:

Toxic relationships

Unproductive relationships

Holding grudges/Unforgiveness

Too much television and not enough books (READ)

Building someone else's dream life (HA!)

Being a "consumer" instead of a "producer"

Settling for less…

Being in the wrong church (you're NOT growing/evolving)

Waiting on other people to affirm and validate your worth

Clothes, shoes, jewelry, hair, nails, travel and you DON'T have life insurance

Chasing people who are not interested in a GENUINE relationship with you

LIFE IS SHORT! Is abundance, compassion, and authenticity with yourself first, then others, how you are living? Live every, single day like it is your last day - because one day it will be!

AUTHENTICITY

"We live in God.
We move in God.
We exist and have our BEING in God."
Acts 17:28

Who are you when no one else is around? That - is an indication of your true self. What is your authenticity statement? Do you have one?

Here is mine:

I believe that every woman is my reflection. The moment you embrace and accept who you are, and all that has happened in your life, is the moment you tap into your authentic soul power to live an amazing life. I believe in having fun, laughing (a lot), dancing (as much as possible), being true to my heart, making a difference and leaving people better than when they met me. And, I believe in loving with every fiber of my being. My life is my message.

My life philosophy includes the following: Loyalty is paramount. Family is always first. Self-care is crucial. Authenticity rocks. Hugs do a body good. Smiles make it better. If it is not fun don't do it for long. There is always a way. Simple is better. When you don't know what to do, follow peace. Nothing is what it seems, go deeper. Live full, die empty. When I am done, I am done. You can love more than one person at a time. Relationships drive your experience. Love is the best thing, yet it is not always enough to sustain a healthy relationship.

I challenge you to write your own authenticity statement and then do your best to live by it daily.

What do I love? I love the beach, a good movie, great music, swimming, reading picture frames, greeting cards, taking care of my plants, beautiful art, travel, charming hotels, amusement parks, good people; essential oils, incense, and sacred sisterhood.

How do others see me? When I have asked others to describe me, they have used these words: authentic, inspiring, motivational, disruptor, connector, friend, caring, compassionate, generous, consistent, reliable, disciplined, intelligent, brilliant, direct, honest, no nonsense, resilient, down to earth, fun, loving, content, aware, evolved, transparent, patient, impactful, relatable, visionary, thoughtful and spiritual.

SOUL WEALTH AFFIRMATIONS FOR AUTHENTICITY

Those in authentic relationship with me know that I am extremely unassuming. I intentionally don't lead with my title, my resume, my bio, or my credentials; and I don't name drop. I am heart-centered, compassionate, generous, observant, kind and very protective of my circle. I'm grateful to be this way. Consequently, when people throw shade or are condescending or don't engage me because they don't see the value or possibilities of the relationship - I am VERY okay with that revelation. It just means you are not my tribe! It cracks me up when people suddenly become friendly after discovering who I am. "No thanks. I am good, Ma'am. I am good, Sir." Life is too short to spend energy trying to impress people who are NOT interested. Moreover, it is why scripture admonishes us to be careful how we entertain strangers because that person you don't know just might be who God sent to bless you. Clarity is a beautiful thing!

This will help a lot of you if you take heed like yesterday. STOP expecting from people what is not in them to give you. Some people honestly don't have the capacity to do, give or be more. Conversely, STOP promising stuff you know you're not going to do. Be impeccable with your word and most importantly just be honest with yourself first! There is a flow to authenticity.

AUTHENTICITY is when you CONSISTENTLY embody the words you speak. Sacred sisterhood is REAL to me. That is AUTHENTICITY! For us to become our most genuine self, we usually must experience a tremendous breakdown or breakup in order to breakthrough. Why? Because devastation will teach you what your ego won't let you learn an easier way. A mess is part of the process to greatness. If you've gone through something that felt like - or you are in something that feels like it's killing you - you're right. The good news is this is a dying of a different k ind; d eath to t he o ld, people-pleasing, counterfeit you so that the - this is who I really am, authentic, on purpose, full of life, I was born to live THIS way you can abound!

One of the most beautiful and amazing things in life is CHOICE! If you don't like your life make different decisions. Your life is currently the result of your choices. You are empowered, anointed and qualified to CREATE the life you desire. To make room for *that life* you must release people, places, memories and things that no longer fit the paradigm of your dream. Go with the flow of what you know is calling you higher. You can do this! You are that powerful!

This is for YOU who are anointed, gifted, talented, qualified, experienced yet feel invisible around people who are familiar with your capacity. My offering to you is travel, meet new people, stretch out of your comfort zone, do something different. Maybe where you currently are people are indifferent. I promise you there are people in the world waiting for you to show up with your gift, your voice, your skill set, your capacity to celebrate and value all of you. Maybe you're just doing the right things around the wrong people in the wrong places.

STOP IT with this hocus pocus, watered - down, conference, collaboration, prophecy chasing, posturing, pretending to be okay display of success and happiness all over social media. It is not real and creates a false sense of unattainability for others. Peace IS possible. People of integrity do exist. However, the truth is many are broken, sufferin in silence and barely making it. The people many are trying to impress don't care and the people who really care are concerned. For every minute in the spotlight it requires 59 minutes of facing truth, sitting in your issues, cutting off toxic people, forgiving self and others, recovering from disappointment, betrayal, obstacles, illusions and just straight up being accountable to someone you trust to support your journey toward healing in the light and spirit of truth. The flip side is the FRAUDULENT display of relationship and what is required to have a seat at the table. The TRUTH is many people ONLY hook up or help people they know or get in vicinity of people who have something they want. This is true in the marketplace AND in many church circles. I can't take it anymore in silence without pulling back the curtain to tell you that what you are chasing will never be caught. You are better than that and worthy of authentic, genuine connec-tion. Know this -- life is so fragile that every, single one of us is ONE EVENT away from life being vastly different. Be a good steward of the opportunities God trusts you to manage. Answer the call on your life so God can bless the world through your gifts. BE AUTHENTIC in every area of your life. From a heart centered place of love – this needed to be said.

Eliminate overwhelm by only committing to things that deeply resonate with who you are authentically.

YOU MUST CHOOSE TO MOVE FORWARD! It's a decision not a feeling. Well-known author and life coach Martha Beck says, "Too much attachment to the past will cause you to get lost in silence and suffering." That's true. Longing for what was but you can't have will make you SUFFER! Sentiment will kill you slowly. Move forward Loved Ones. That's where you can find joy again, love and be loved again, discover better, create again, smile again, laugh again. There

Soul Wealth

is nothing behind you that you've lost that is necessary for your pres-ent or future, EXCEPT gratitude for the experience. It was a lesson to grow you forward. Don't feel sorry for yourself that you lost it or them. Be grateful that you had the opportunity to learn from it. You are ALREADY better because of it.

When I think back on the people - pleasing, never ending quest to be liked and included in what I thought was the "in crowd" it inspires me to live an even more UN-OFFENDED life. When I tell you, I am free and unattached from what people think about me now - please believe - I AM CO-DEPENDENT NO MORE!!! What is it? It is when dysfunctional people become worse together. That's right, God blocked a lot of those connections. Some of the people I wanted so badly to accept me are still stuck in what I thought was or where I wanted to be. Whew! I'm not angry either. As a matter of fact, I am grateful because I understand that the bondage experience is necessary to manage freedom properly. Psychology Today says you are well on your way to recovery when: You nurture your own wants and desires and develop a connection to your inner world. You see yourself as reliant, smart, and capable. You say goodbye to abusive behavior. Awareness, change, and growth are necessary for you to overcome un-healthy relationship habits. You respond instead of reacting to others. Setting clear, firm boundaries means you don't automatically react to everyone's thoughts and feelings. You tolerate other people's opinions and do not become defensive when you disagree. You recognize that your reaction is your responsibility. You adopt a healthy skepticism about what others say about you (good or bad), and your self-esteem doesn't rise and fall as a result. You say no, and you accept hearing no. My mission in the marketplace is to inspire as many people (especially women) to join me on this journey of non-attached living. If it is your desire to live an authentic and unattached life YET be filled with love, peace and happiness then WRITE IN THE SPACE PROVIDED BELOW... "I AM manifesting in every area of my life."

_____

It's amazing how when you SLOW DOWN and align yourself with what you know God called you to do that things you used to dream of going after start LOOKING FOR YOU!

If you're going to worry, then don't pray. If you're going to pray, then don't worry. Shift your posture to one of it's already done; and the how - well leave that up to God!

No makeup! No filter! No worries! NONE! Wear the smirk of PEACE and FREEDOM knowing that the Word of God is true. Better is the end of a thing than its beginning. It hasn't even entered your heart the GREATER things that God has in store for you.

The day
#SoulWealth
was born.

I REALLY
am a
beach
baby!

I've been a beach baby all my life. I wasn't too happy with my big brother in this picture.

I'm smiling, but I was actually sad. I was so unsure of myself while at Seminole Middle School.

This accident almost left me crippled. It took me a year to learn how to walk again. BUT GOD!

I love this classic b/w photo of me. I was still searching for clarity of my purpose.

Rocking
my fierce
short
hair cut.

In 2013, I hosted
Girl Talk
Unplugged:
The Ultimate
Getaway. It was a
pivotal moment
for me. This is a
power shot of
attendees.

I love being
a woman!
Femininity
is a beautiful
thing.

Officiating
weddings is
one of my
favorite
things to
do.

Finally HER!
I love this
power pose in
all white.

Rocking my
signature
braids just
before a
speaking
engagement.

This is the day I knew in my soul that I was born to help women heal!

Here I was 100% sure I had an anointing for marketplace impact.

ABUNDANCE

*"Now to Him who by the power at work within
us is able to accomplish abundantly far more
than we can ask or imagine."*
Ephesians 3:20

Overflow! Overflow is abundance. I often say, "Your capacity is for you and your overflow is the well from which you quench the thirst of others." Once you maintain your capacity on a consistent basis you create fertile ground for overflow and abundance. Abundance shows up in our lives when we have done the work to heal emotionally, mentally, spiritually, relationally and physically. Your life follows your words. The most powerful tool of creating abundance is our thoughts. Yes, our lives follow our words, but our words follow our thoughts.

Consistency of the right thoughts and actions produces abundance too. A confused mind does nothing, attracts nothing but chaos and wastes a lot of time. Focus also unlocks the door to abundance. Peace and abundance go together. Again, a confused mind does nothing and neither does an anxious mind. God's desire for us is great peace. God's desire for us is blessings without sorrow. God's desire for us is life more abundantly so we can live in peace.

I always knew I would live a life of abundance. I've known since I was a child, that overflow, or abundance was my destiny. It is why I love the beach so much. The vastness of the ocean is a metaphor of God's intention of abundance for each of us. I love nice things. I love to travel. I love to engage in cultural experiences that soothe the soul. I love good music. I love art. My relationships are blessed relationships.

I share my garden of abundance because I also believe you don't have to suffer or settle for sandpaper on your soul to have nice things, a nice life or quality relationships. You do not have to sell your soul to have abundance. In fact, you must settle your soul to have abundance in every area of your life. A life filled with an abundance of love, joy, peace, favor and light is your birthright.

SOUL WEALTH AFFIRMATIONS FOR ABUNDANCE

Don't be attached to what you think you see or hear. Seek the wisdom of God FIRST about everything. Pray without ceasing. Whatever happens ~ trust in the Lord with all your heart! Don't lean to your own understanding. In all your ways acknowledge Him, lead with gratitude, agree with God quickly and the PEACE OF GOD will guard your heart, your mind, your spirit, your emotions, your way."

I had never seen anything like this in person before. To sit and watch 20-foot waves dance was powerful! Then God said, "Get ready for it ~ you're about to see many things you've never seen before that are breathtaking!" At that very moment a whale and two dolphins swam by!

When you focus on alignment then Psalm 133:3 says, "From that place called UNITY you can command blessings and attract perpetual peace."

Though a large part of the country was in shock and discouraged after the election of Donald Trump as President of the United States; I realized that the anointing of Issachar is real. And in all honesty, we should be excited about the four years he would serve in that position! God takes the foolish things of this world to confound the wise and what appears weak will be given wisdom to overtake and/or find opportunities in that which declares strength. I admonish you in the seasons of shock and discouragement to take your moments to process what you are feeling -THEN - get busy. Faith without works is dead AND favor is still following you!

This is NOT the season to get off track. You must be focused, disciplined and paying attention to what's going on in you and around you. The windows of opportunity that God is presenting will be quick, so be steadfast. Get your life, heart, mind, money, relationships in order so God can blow your mind. It's happening now! God is releasing uncommon and unexpected favor in unexpected places.

Each of us was born with a witty invention ~ not one person was left out. You are one idea away from the LIFESTYLE of your dreams, whatever it is! The difference between those who live like this and those who don't is a decision to go for it. Success is failure turned inside out! I am living my dreams daily and you can too.

Soul Abundance is possible! I am a witness that doubt, cynicism, fear and settling is overrated. What is your vision? What is your dream? What are you waiting for? Only give access to those who believe what you believe is possible! Everyone else can watch!

I'm learning daily that there are times in life when God must withhold the details of your glorious, wonderful future to protect you! I now understand clearly, I'm not for everybody and everybody is not for me. However, there IS a people waiting for my voice, my story, my gifts. Same is true for YOU if you're reading this. Stop trying to force your way into spaces that don't fit and therefore don't feel good. They are NOT your tribe. Be authentic and BE okay with that...REAL TALK! The process of maturity is not just to perfect your character but to purge the people from your life who would ONLY stay connected to have access to the amazing things coming your way. Loved Ones there are people you haven't met yet and rooms you've not experienced yet that are going to BLOW YOUR MIND! What you have left is more than enough and what's headed your way is so much better than what's been. YES - it gets better.

It is important in all things to treat people the way you want to be treated. PERIOD. Some people only know how to celebrate and show up for you when you are broken, struggling, suffering, in your process or having some difficulty. When the tables start to turn ~ (which they always, eventually do) ~ and your season starts to shift to one of "better days", pay attention to the people who become intolerant of your presence now that you don't need their assistance. Don't be discouraged, dismayed or discontent however…be grateful for the lessons learned and be clear. It's not personal it's purposeful. You don't have to tolerate being disrespected to prove that you respect and honor someone. When you start to ascend and transcend you must travel lightly. There are people you haven't met yet, waiting to celebrate you where you are going. Sit with that Loved Ones and let it bless you.

COR-NU-CO-PI-A ~ An abundant supply of good things of a spec-ified kind; an ocean; a wealth of; LOTS; a heap; millions; loads; plentifulness; a bounty; an amplitude; lavishness. HA! Sounds like Soul Wealth and Soul Abundance to me!

God will make you fruitful again in every place of failure. The turn that is coming will be PERFECT for you.

Sometimes God keeps you in obscurity during the process to perfect you for what's coming. The results will prove that FAVOR was sent before you to make room for you in rooms that will blow your mind and bless your life. THIS IS WHY YOU MUST NOT GIVE UP!

Be okay with being different! God made us the way we are for a reason and plans to use every quirky thing about us. At the same time, allow and accept other people's right to be who they are. The beautiful thing is that we get to decide if we want to deal with them or not. Either way is fine. God doesn't micromanage people and neither should we. The moment we decide to live this way is the moment we step into perpetual peace!

By now some things ought not to bother you the way they used to. By now you should have moved on to something healthier since you have new information. By now you should be testifying not still complaining. By now your challenges should be different because you are now in another dimension of illumination. By now you should be manifesting results and having eternal impact in the earth. By now you should be encouraging others by speaking life not draining the life out of people you have access to. By now your language should be one of victory not that of victimhood. By now you should have decided not to still be wavering in indecision. By now someone who loves you should have told you they love you too much to let you stay stuck in sameness, brokenness, excuseness *(made that up)* and lameness. God is GREAT in us, through us, as us! You are too anointed to be impotent! By this time next year, don't be the same broken person, in the same stale place, doing the same ineffective, non-productive thing. I LOVE YOU and YOU ARE BETTER THAN THAT!

PROPHETIC INTERRUPTION: You are NOT responsible for other people's happiness. Stop delaying your joy because they" are miserable. The best gift you can give them is to be happy in your happiness anyway. Get back to your life NOW - right now!

While out running several errands one day I noticed a pattern that I believe will bless you. While completing my first stop I was in/out in two minutes. I thought "Wow that was easy!" Next stop in/out five minutes. I thought, "God this is awesome!" Stop after that, what usually takes about 45 minutes, took 15 minutes. I thought, "God you are really showing off today." Final stop, typically there is a line, but I was the only one in the building being serviced so it was beyond pleasant and painless. I thought, "Something has definitely shifted in the atmosphere." PROPHETIC OBSERVATION: The things in your immediate or long term past that have been a struggle, that have been delayed, that have caused frustration or been a major irritation ARE NOW easy, available, and sources of joy!!!

I was walking on the beach admiring a lovely rooftop and suddenly realized that it was also the first floor of another building. Then God said, "Just like that EVERY ceiling in your life has become the floor of your next level!" If you are reading this - that goes for you too! It's called spiritual growth and Soul Wealth.

I am at peace with being different! I know and am confident that when those feelings of wanting to fade to the background come up ~ just like back then ~ I can lean in and trust that God is STILL transforming what's awkward into something awesome! From awkward to awesome!

Sometimes God allows some obstacles, situations, challenges, hard-ships to linger longer than we want. Usually it is to teach us to trust the process and the power of surrender. Know that WHEN God says so - that thing - will be handled just like that. The solution always has an appointed time. Is there anything too hard for God?

No, there is nothing. Be anxious for nothing. BREATHE. When you least expect it God will show up strong for YOU with yet another victory!

This is a genuine observation (as I don't give advice). BUILD GENUINE RELATIONSHIPS! The fake and the faux are tem-porary. Stop giving so much to people who are so BOLD they only give you the time of day when they want something! End up in the hospital, lose a Loved One, get laid off your job, experience a hard-ship and you will see who is really for you. Invest in your family, the people who have invested in you when you had nothing and in the less fortunate, disenfranchised (like the homeless, the children, the elderly). Trust me on this ~ people MAKE TIME for who and what they really want in their sacred space.

While the process of ascending to your highest self can be quite pain-ful, the payoff will be worth it. The purging and emptying of what no longer serve you is uncomfortable. Take good notes (journal) while *going through it* so that WHEN you *come out* you can refer to what you learned about yourself AND others. Not sure who this is for but Loved One, YOU are almost out, and the struggle IS over! PEACE IS POSSIBLE!

Doors of tremendous opportunity have opened for you that are out-side of your comfort zone and current qualifications. Say YES. Don't resist or sabotage or allow fear to keep you from these blessings. You are qualified! You have within what you need to be effective and in-fluential. Your life is about to change again; in major ways. I have been pondering this for some time. I'm inspired to share it to-day because I know I am not the only who is tired.

I am tired of the rat race. I am tired of watching people struggle to live less than authentic lives. I am tired of watching women compete, compare and conspire to outdo each other. I am tired of people who are up today mistreat other people, forgetting that one day the tables will turn. I am tired of people not keeping their word. I am tired of the oppressive, dogmatic world systems (political, educational, corporate, religious, prison in-dustrial complex) that subliminally suppress the masses into living on automatic pilot. I am tired of racism, police brutality, black on black crime, senseless violence, poverty and all that comes with these issues. I am tired; YET not without hope! Decide to spend the rest of your life living from your overflow not your capacity. Loved Ones SLOW DOWN; spend time in sacred, peaceful spaces that fill you up; take deep, cleansing breaths often; pray without ceasing; drink more water; spend time near water; and nurture the relationships that matter most. FILL YOUR CUP; because you can't give away what you don't have. Feel your feelings fully! We were born into this world with nothing, we accumulate a lot of stuff, issues, wounds (sometimes we come here with it) then spend the rest of our lives trying to get rid of it all. This is a clarion call to Soul Wealth so you can truly live in perpetual abundance.

God speaks to me in the most uncommon ways! Was having what I'll call some technology challenges and when I picked up one of my de-vices it said, "REBOOT AND RECOVER ALL!" I started running in my mind! Loved Ones - EVERY SYSTEM in your life is being rearranged in your favor!

DO NOT PANIC! Something beyond your reach in the natural is on its way to you in the supernatural. Stay ready. It is coming soon. Read it again and again.

There was a time that I felt weirdly unaffected by anything. That's the best way to describe what I was experiencing. I didn't really feel like talking much or being around a lot of people. If I allowed myself, I would be easily irritated; so, solitude really helped to manage that place of what I couldn't explain until – one night. I said out loud, "I FEEL LIKE I'M IN LABOR, ABOUT TO GIVE BIRTH!" God whispered and said, "You are in labor and it's time to push!" Loved Ones I am sharing because just maybe someone else has felt the same unexplainable emotions. You can do this too. Remember to breathe then push a little more. The discomfort is temporary. What's about to come out of you is going to be beautiful and it's going to CHANGE YOUR LIFE FOR THE BETTER FOREVER! Now unto Him who is able to do exceeding abundantly above all that we can ask or think! It's about to be laughing season!

IT IS WAITING FOR YOU! Had the awesome pleasure of taking my daughter to the MARC Train Station for her daily commute. If you are NOT on the platform when this train pulls up, you will get left and must wait for the next one. We saw the train and she said, "It's okay, I'll catch the next train." However, I felt the need to press so she could catch that one. Well God broke the rule that morning. Not only was the train already at the station, but the crew was standing on the platform as if they were waiting for her. They even teased her saying, "RUN FASTER!" She made the train AND got a seat. Y'all know I got a revelation, right? There are some promises with YOUR name on them that God is holding up just for your arrival. Don't draw back! You are closer than you think to the manifestation of what God said. PRESS ON ~ every, single promise God made IS WAITING FOR YOU!!!!

LEGACY

*"I will make you an object of pride forever and
joy from generation to generation."*
Isaiah 60:15

"A good man leaves an inheritance to his children's children.
Proverbs 13:22

This happened while I was writing this book:

> **"Hi Vikki, The City Council voted on Monday and
> the home is officially an Orlando Local Landmark.
> Thank you for all your assistance with the appli-
> cation and know that your grandfather's home is
> recognized as a landmark for its association with
> Pappy Kennedy and all his wonderful accomplish-
> ments. I just received the signed ordinance for the
> Mayor's office."**

As I ponder the season I am currently living in, what resonates most is my desire to leave a tangible and intangible legacy for my daughter, nieces, nephews, godchildren and the women who have entrusted me as a mentor. As a matter of fact, the same day I received the above notification, is the same day I received the cover layout for this book (which I absolutely love)! It really captures the essence of Soul Wealth and everything I love. It is a visual metaphor of chaos (the waves behind me) contrasted against vision, compassion, authenticity, abundance and legacy (reflected in my wind-blown hair, white dress and peace on my face) while sitting in the sand.

I don't believe it was ever God's intention for every generation to start from the bottom. For as long as I can remember, I have heard if you want to understand where you are going you must understand, honor and respect where you came from. I am not just from Fort Lauderdale, Florida (proud of this fact by the way). I am also from a colorful, powerful, purpose driven lineage of Cherokee, Creek, Nigerian, Sierra Leone, Jamaican, Georgian, South Carolinian, Floridian ancestors who sacrificed what they did so that I could be who I am. They were preachers, teachers, entrepreneurs, homemakers, longshoremen, corporate executives, elected officials, healers, members of the military, poets, singers, revolutionaries, Christian, Muslim, Yoruba, water and nature lovers.

Legacy is about those that come behind you being able to "stand on the shoulders" of your success so that they start building their legacy from a better place. How will you be remembered? What will people say about you when you are no longer here? Do you know who you are and where you come from? Go on a journey to discover these things so you can begin living your legacy now.

Start right now. Decide to create a tangible and intangible legacy. What character traits do you want others to emulate? Decide now to buy land/property. Ensure that you take care of those that love you by having life insurance in place. Beyond life insurance contact an attorney to set up a living trust for the preservation, protection and distribution of your assets. You may be thinking, "I don't have any assets." That is okay too, because you can begin creating an inheritance now. Do you have a fire proof safe in your home for important documents? Are you taking care of your body? Are you managing relationships properly? Are you having conversations with family members and people you trust about your desires for life after you are gone? This is Soul Wealth! Get your business straight. It starts with a decision.

My paternal Grandfather was the first African American, elected official in the city of Orlando, Florida. Growing up my siblings and cousins spent at least two weeks every summer with our Grandparents. We had fun and we had chores. We had three meals a day which included dinner together as a family every day. After saying grace, we each had to say a bible verse before we ate. I can remember how we all wanted to go first so we could recite "Jesus wept" because it was the shortest verse in the Bible. That makes me laugh today!

My paternal Grandmother was an amazing cook. She was a tall, stately, soft spoken woman of great grace and character. Our Grandfather was a short, handsome man who was deeply passionate about community, family and loved God. He would end every conversation with "don't forget to pray." I remember him running for political office in the 70s. I remember him winning. He passed down his love for politics to my father, who after many years as an educator, became entrenched in national politics as Chief of Staff to a United States Congressman. After serving in this role for some 30 years, he finally retired from that position in his 80s because he loved it so much. You see when you do what you love it doesn't feel like work.

My maternal Grandparents were just as awesome. We spent holidays and many Sunday afternoons at their house. One of my favorite memories of my maternal Grandmother was her Avon room. Another favorite memory is the delicious food that always seemed to be on her stove no matter what day or time of day. She was the vocal one in her home, church and community. My passion for empowering women came from her. Because of her I started my first girls' club at 10 years old called the Clover Zodiacs. My Mother was our advisor - LOL. I am still friends with these girls (now women) to this day. I am named after her mother (my Great Grandmother) whose name was Victoria. My maternal Grandfather was a longshoreman. My uncles, cousins and siblings followed in his footsteps (legacy). Some of them still work at the port today. He was a handsome man of few words and he loved his family. I am blessed that I was able to have relationship with both sets of grandparents.

My parents are phenomenal too! I had a wonderful childhood that prepared me to live the life I live today. Before I completed writing this book, I was able to see the Mayor of City of Orlando publicly declare that my Grandparents' home is officially an Orlando Historic Landmark! The beauty is I am still living and building my legacy of Soul Wealth and teaching others to do the same.

SOUL WEALTH AFFIRMATIONS FOR LEGACY

Think about the circumstance and situations over the course of your life where the exactitude of God made the difference. In those moments the right people were in the right place with precisely what you needed to manifest the victory. Victory can look like varying things! Victory is not always having the most points on the board, making the most money or outdoing your opponents. Sometimes victory is simply God's grace keeping you from losing your mind, not fainting in your heart or spirit or falling to pieces when your reality may merit such. The peace of God is the greatest gift ever!!! Because God is - I AM TOO!

Some know me as Vikki, others as "Elder Vikki", and to some amazing men whom I still love dearly they say, "she used to be MY GIRL" (lol)!I love the beach, the spa, music, sistHERhood, spending time with good friends, family, laughing, helping others, photography, and DANCING! I'm loving, generous, shy (believe it or not), giving, a bottom-line person, and very pensive. If you cross or betray me, let's just say it will only happen once. I've had some very painful times and some defining, unforgettable moments that have shaped who I am. I am here to SERVE! I believe that every woman is me and I am her. I started Girl Talk Unplugged A Sacred Sisterhood 13 years ago, so I speak, write, coach and share from experience! My daughter is my reason for blazing trails. I do, so she can, just like my Grandmothers, Great Grandmothers, Aunts, and Mom did for me. To me, loyalty is paramount, self-care is crucial, hugs are good for the soul, love deeply or not at all, every experience is a classroom, mediocre is whack, conscious living is important, nothing is what it seems. God is always in the details and kindness is free. "I'm Every Woman" is my theme song, chocolate cake is my favorite dessert and I love being a girl. I'm a proud member of Delta Sigma Theta Sorority, National Association of Black Female Executives in Music & Entertainment (NABFEME), and am surrounded by phenomenal coaches, mentors and other women leaders. I am drawn to what feels good to ME! I love nice things, nice people, nice places, and am a hotel snob (proud of it). LAUGHTER IS MANDATORY! As an athlete who played basketball for years, I'm a team player and a connector. I'm sexy, sensual, spiritual, and sophisticated YET down to earth. I like walking barefoot on the beach. My love language is quality time and touch (for sure). The lotus flower is my favorite flower because its beauty rises out of the muck and mire. At this point in my life, I only care to deal with what really matters to me. Everything else is a distraction. The best part of this journey called life is the opportunity to ***pour out*** all that God has entrusted to me.

Sometimes in quiet reflection I ask God why did He make me the way that I am? Why do I love people? Particularly why is "sacred sisterhood" so important to me? Why am I such a nurturer? Why am I so committed to the underdog? Why do I give so much? Why do I care so deeply? Why does He open my "spiritual eyes" to see so far into the future and others have no clue or perception? Why am I on this path? The answer so sweetly entered my heart. "There remains a rest in the place of transcendent living! TRUST ME!" That's all God said - LOL!!! There is a promise attached to your life Loved Ones that's GREATER than you imagine. Where God guides provision is already there. TRUST GOD! One thing I know for sure...GOD IS...able to - (YOU get to fill in the blank)!!!

I was pondering things deeply planted in my heart. Believe it or not I've never really FELT like I "fit in" anywhere or with any group of people. Hence, I spend a lot of time alone and I'm genuinely okay with that. It's why I love the water so much. I've always felt just slightly outside the circle or that I had to do extra special things to really be accepted. I used to resent being gifted or having the mind of a trailblazer because honestly it can be very lonely. Not lonely in the sense of I don't have friends (because I have amazing people in my life) ~ but lonely in the sense of being in a crowd yet still feeling alone. God has given me ideas that are decades before their time. I'd try them with what I considered reasonable effect. However, they weren't what I considered *good enough* to keep as a priority, so I let them go only to see the same concept YEARS later explode into massive success. What I now understand is that successful people are those who kept rising after falling. Everything that has happened in my life has brought me to this place of undisturbed composure called SOUL WEALTH!!! I will no longer apologize for being awesome! I will no longer dim my light so other people can be okay! I will no longer do things or say yes to things I don't really want to do! I will no longer be silent, so I don't hurt feelings even though my feelings were hurt. I have stepped through and into a portal of God that will manifest unapologetic impact in the earth…all for God's glory. I'm so grateful for the illumination of this fact: THE THINGS THAT MAKE YOU WEIRD ARE THE THINGS THAT ALSO MAKE YOU WONDERFULLY YOU!

When you're disingenuous it's really obvious! Trying to be like others or liked by others is overrated when it's not from a place of authenticity. When you really "show up" in the world and manifest who God called you to be there will be people who walk away from you because your magnificence will be too bright. Let them! The beautiful thing is that same light and brilliance will attract the people who will celebrate, support, pour into you (not just take all the time), and believe in you so amazingly that one day it will hit you…what took me so long to get here.

How about living (daily) according to your vision and not from a place of fear or lack? Live your life so completely that when you die… you're empty!

I have learned SO many lessons. To sum it up lovingly, God's plan is so much bigger than our pain, chaos, betrayal, confusion, being left out, looked over, mistreated or mishandled. Even when we don't un-derstand it, God knows the thoughts and plans He has for us…never to harm us but to give us hope and an expected end. Worth repeating ~ God's plan for our lives is SO much bigger than our pain. It is shift shaping for your soul!

The older I get the lighter I feel! I'm vehemently committed to "having a life" not just making a living. I used to make choices first considering how others would be impacted then how it would affect me. I don't do that anymore because too often I was left with not much or nothing. I've learned to give to givers not to takers. There must be reciprocity in my relationships, or I choose to relate from a distance. It's a new month, new season, new day and life is good. Don't be afraid to allow your intimate circle to shrink. Life is about quality not quantity! Continue dancing, laughing, loving and spending as much time as possible at the beach.

As an avid swimmer and lover of water I've learned over the years that when you go with the current it's easier to move. Such is life! Stop creating drama where there is none. Stop looking for the struggle because you're used to things being hard. God has set you in a NEW PLACE! Believe it! Go with the flow and enjoy the ease of God!

Integrity preserves. However, the lack of integrity will destroy you.

I took a few moments one day to stare at a photograph of myself and was flooded with GRATITUDE! Although I'm smiling on the photo it was an incredibly sad time in my life. I was dealing with postpartum depression! While my daughter brought and still brings me immense joy, some days back then, I was barely functioning. GOD KEPT ME TOGETHER when I was literally making it moment by moment on broken pieces. Stop making assumptions about people and pray for them, be nice to them, offer compassion, show love. I thank God for the people who surrounded me and, on many days, unknowingly "saved my life" with a smile, a hug, a card or phone call.

Where you are is not all there is to your life. There is more. Your best days are ahead of you. You will be happy again. There is a place in God (in you) where your joy is not predicated on your circumstances. Remember to breathe and if you must ~ borrow hope from me until your well becomes full. Soul Wealth is REAL. Trust the process.

You can be in a hard place for so long that you get stuck with a mind-set of struggle, disappointment and low expectations...even after the season has shifted toward better. Loved Ones, sometimes you must stand in the mirror, get indignant with yourself and command your soul to embrace the breakthrough!

Don't make people who are available to love you now suffer because of people who were not available to love you back then.

Soul Wealth is the manifestation of my personal healing journey. It didn't happen overnight. It has been a long time coming. Do your work. Trust the process.

Life would be so much easier for us all if we would simply do the right thing! If you have an issue, please say something. If you're in pain get support. If you are no longer interested don't do it anymore. If the relationship isn't nurturing or edifying, get out. If you make a commitment keep it or don't make it. Just do what you say you're going to do. Stop making promises and not keeping them. The Golden Rule is still applicable. "Do unto others as you would have them do unto you." If you know you wouldn't like it done to you don't do it to others.

Get to the point (just decide) that you will not waste another heartbeat or moment of your life trying to please people who are not able to be pleased! Life is too short. My Dad says all the time, "Tough times don't last but tough people do." Keep your heart open and trust in the Lord with ALL your heart. Your destiny is controlled by your agreement with God alone (Job 22). People don't have that much power. STAY FOCUSED!!! What you are going through didn't come to stay - it came to pass. STAY FOCUSED, do your part and God will do the rest!

For you who are waiting on a breakthrough, hang in there. My travels often produce insight that I love sharing. Recently, I was on a flight that took off in the rain, ascended to 40-thousand feet, then landed in the sunshine!!! God just gave you a preview of what's coming. DON'T QUIT!

PROPHETIC EXHORTATION: God is never surprised nor reactionary. Therefore, don't you be surprised or reactionary either. Be sober, vigilant and anxious for nothing.

Don't be attached to what you think you see or hear. Seek the wisdom of God FIRST about everything. Pray without ceasing. Whatever happens ~ trust in the Lord with all your heart! Don't lean to your own understanding. In all your ways acknowledge Him, lead with gratitude, agree with God quickly and the PEACE OF GOD will guard your heart, your mind, your spirit, your emotions, your way.

Many people suffer from chronic disappointment. On every level I have had my share of being let down by people I trusted to never let me fall. It can be quite debilitating, paralyzing, a justifiable cause of procrastination and at times a reason to feel like giving up. I know this place very well. I'm sharing to encourage you to take a deep breath then exhale as many times as you must to get a second wind. Over time I have learned you have to be willing to lose to win. Quite often it is in losing one job that you discover a more lucrative way to make a living. You may have to lose some friends to win others. In some cases, you must lose a love to experience the "love of your life." You may have to lose what's familiar to win better ~ often in the unknown. Sometimes you must be willing to give up what you have to gain what you want. I'm just saying, sometimes you must LOSE YOURSELF TO FIND YOURSELF!

PARADOX OF BEING GIFTED is a reality for many. While your gift brings you before greatness it is often difficult to discern who is who. Unfortunately, ***authentic relationships*** for gifted people are a challenge because when "the gift" (influence, access, advantage) is no longer useful or needed the relationship disappears. This is painful.

Just because people celebrate the benefit of your gift doesn't qualify them for intimate access to who you are as a person. I have learned this lesson several times and that's why I'm sharing. **Divine connections** endure seasons! Stop giving away everything to people who do not have the capacity to honor YOU and your gift. Who is there when the applause stops? Really think about that and then invest in those relationships. What you have left is enough to preserve proven relationships in your life. Keep your heart open; there is more sweetness headed your way! I see you and you are loved!

The older I get the more valuable the phrase: "If it doesn't fit don't force it" becomes. I am not just over but beyond working hard to make relationships work. I show up the way I expect to be treated. I will not chase. I will not seek to impress. I will not over give any longer to influence an outcome. I will love from a distance and be content. When people show me who they are I choose to believe them. Transcendent living is not for the faint of heart! I look for and live in the ease of God!

God blessed me so ridiculously in a 24-hour span that I'm still weepy. While sitting in my "summer office" I began reflecting on all that God has brought me through. In 1991, I had a catastrophic athletic injury that required three surgeries, incredibly challenging rehab, three months on my back, pins/screws literally holding my bones together and then a year to learn to walk again. I looked at ONE of my scars and in my periphery saw the pool. I got weepy again. Here I am sitting in the sun by the pool (something I love) looking at evidence of a memory that no longer hurts. Y'all know I got a message, right? We have just entered a season where the scars remain -BUT

THE PAIN IS GONE! Believe that the pain is gone so you can make room for your joy!!!

It was a Sunday afternoon in June 1991. It was Fathers' Day to be exact. While I was playing softball, another player slid into me while I was covering home plate. He dislocated my ankle, fractured my ankle and shattered my tibia bone. As God would have it on the next field was a group of firefighters playing their own tournament. They heard me screaming and ran over to see what was going on. They took two bats, several gloves and ace bandages to stabilize me. I am so grateful for my angels who stayed with me the entire time. Upon arrival at the ER, via ambulance, the surgeon on call said if I had been in another country, they would have amputated my leg because of the damage. The staff at <u>Washington Adventist Hospital</u> was phenomenally compassionate. They took great care of me. I had two surgeries to reconstruct my leg and ankle, was in the hospital for over a week and had to lay flat for twelve weeks so my bones could fuse back together. I then had to endure therapy for over a year to learn how to walk again. I don't look like what I've been through!!! People see the promise but often don't know the price that was paid. God has been good to me. God is faithful to restore your life after trauma and devastation. I am sharing this because somebody is about to give up. Don't you dare quit! Your broken places are becoming your places of blessing. MORAL OF STORY: After all this God healed me to the point that I don't even have a limp! This is why I dance, why I praise. My story is a wonder!

CONCLUSION

How do you live so that others remember you? You build a **legacy** one encounter at a time. You must intend to leave a life changing, positive impression on every person that crosses your path.

Once you become a person of **vision** it unlocks your **compassion**. Living from a place of consistent practice with showing yourself empathy, support, love, grace and care will ignite you to do the same for others. You cannot give away what you don't have. You cannot effectively demonstrate for others what is not activated in your life first. You can only pretend for so long. Eventually you will burn out or wear out or be found out.

Authenticity comes from following your heart again and again and again. It comes from being true to your desires and true to the impressions God has placed on your heart. Having a clear picture of your likes, dislikes, beliefs, convictions and core values builds character. It also strengthens your integrity muscle allowing you to live in and speak your truth even when it makes you uncomfortable. The discomfort, however, is only temporary. The more you practice authentic living the easier it becomes.

The beautiful reality of moving forward and deeper into Soul Wealth is that eventually it unlocks your abundance. You know in your spirit, soul and body when this happens. You live in a perpetual state of peace. You practice being fully present in every moment. You live with no regrets - only lessons. It feels like favor now follows you everywhere you go; and frustration does not last long because your awareness is heightened. You recognize or sense when things are not in alignment and quickly adjust.

Soul Wealth is your birthright. You are worthy of an amazing life - right now. You don't have to wait another moment. Make a decision and then take the correlating action to manifest in your life what you see in your mind. Listen to your heart. Silence the chatter and follow what you know to be your truth.

What if all our disappointment, discouragement, distress, depression, dissonance, differences, delays and detours were simply to get us to experience love? What if all the bad people we thought were going to hell (who transitioned before us) greeted us at Heaven's gate dressed in white, transformed into their divinity? What if every heartbreak was to break us open so the love inside could spill out into the world? I'm just asking questions to provoke you to think beyond any limiting, fear-filled, intimidating beliefs that tell you that you are not worthy of living an amazing life! You are worthy of a beautiful life even if chaos is happening all around you.

Love comes from the inside! WHATEVER is going on in your life simply remember that it is all about getting you to experience love. Don Miguel Ruiz says, ***"It is the love COMING OUT OF YOU that makes you happy!"*** The love you seek you already have in your heart. Release it so you can attract vision, compassion, authenticity, abundance and legacy! By now you should know I am talking about Soul Wealth.

You can't flourish in your flow if you're comparing yourself to others. You can't shine in your flow if you're constantly gathering information and not implementing what you're learning. You can't create the wealth you're worthy of if you're always starting and never finishing. The ideas and blessings attached to your life will never find you if you keep playing small, dimming your light, and doubting the gifts God gave you. You're hiding if you always talk yourself out of investing in your personal growth. A slight shift from "being intimidated by the cost" TO "assessing the value" of a thing will exponentially SHIFTSHAPE your life in every way. What are you supposed to be doing right now that excuses have kept you from doing? There is ALWAYS a way and as shared before, life is a series of decisions! Pay attention to the signs all around you.

Despite all the craziness going on in the world, **GREAT THINGS** are manifesting. We just must **stay in alignment with God and self.** Don't allow life and other people's drama to make you cynical or jaded. Find beauty in simple things. Intend to be peaceful and remain undisturbed. **Spend time with people who challenge you and make you better.** Learn something new. Perpetual joy is available to you when you make room for it. Your dreams are en route; so, get ready. It is happening. Start from where you are right now and make the rest of your days the absolute best. SOUL WEALTH is real and available for every area of your life.

ABOUT THE AUTHOR

Dr. Vikki Johnson started Girl Talk Unplugged in 1999 and has since transformed the lives of over a half million women. Her passion for empowering women has evolved into SOUL WEALTH - a lifestyle brand! Today, the "Soul Wealth Sacred Sisterhood" nurtures women leaders globally helping them build their own communities of sacred sisterhood. She mentors women to be great in the mirror fir st, then amazing in the marketplace.

An Emmy Award winning media professional with almost 40 years in entertainment & 20 years in marketplace social impact, she had a successful 18-year career at BET Networks. A graduate of Howard University, she is a proud member of Delta Sigma Th e ta Sorority, National Association of Black Female Executives In Music & Entertainment (NABFEME), Women's Speakers Association (WSA) & serves on MC Lyte's Hip Hop Sisters Foundation W.E.A.L.T.H Experience Portal "Spiritual Support Team." Please visit her website www.vikkijohnson.com

SOUL WEALTH SACRED SISTER MANIFESTO

WRITTEN BY SANJO JENDAYI

"True leaders understand that leadership is not about them but about those they serve. It is not about exalting themselves but about lifting others up."
Sheri L. Dew

"Some leaders are born women."
Geraldine Ferraro

Sisterhood: *The SWSS Woman* understands the importance of forming positive relationships with women who have common interest, purpose and whose only fear is mediocrity. She shows up authentically fully aware of her PowHer and uses it wisely. She knows that unity of such women moves mountains!

Sacred Space: *The SWSS Woman* treasures the space this group holds for them, she places high value on what is said, done and experienced within this space and has great respect for its holy energy.

Safe Place: *The SWSS Woman* knows that this is a place where she is free from harm, ridicule, or the threat of danger. She actively listens and shares with confidence affording the same courtesy and confidentiality to her sisters. She will speak in love & truth refusing to offer sugar coated responses. She CAN. SHE WILL. SHE MUST assist in lifting the weight of the illusion of fear from herself and others. She does not just listen hoping and praying that her sister will be okay… she takes an active role in ensuring that it is so.

Spiritual Connection: *The SWSS Woman* is a spiritually awakened woman aware of her energy and the energy around her. She has a connection to the GOD/DESS inside of her which allows her to not only connect with others but to help draw from them the capabilities within them that they may not have known existed. She is spiritually equipped to draw others closer to the GOD/DESS that resides in them. She knows that she is subject to a "bad day" every so often but her faith allows her to turn those dark moments into a light at the end of the tunnel. She uses those days to lay the foundation for her future.

Source of Resources: *The SWSS Woman* recognizes that she is a source of resources for others but more importantly, she isn't prideful or boastful. She effectively utilizes her resourceful sisters to impact the world around her.

Servant Leaders: *The SWSS Woman* operates in humble service. She does not place herself above doing what is necessary to get the job done. She is a true leader who isn't afraid to get in the trenches with those whom she has been charged to lead. She isn't a dictator directing others. She does not desire to create minions; instead she fosters greatness and genius in those around her thereby strengthening leaders for tomorrow.

Synergistic: *The SWSS Woman* increases her own effectiveness by joining forces, gifts and talents with like-minded sisters creating a mutually advantageous team of game changers!

Soulfully Sensuous: *The SWSS Woman* taps into her mind, body & spirit by nourishing her soul through her senses. She has strong sensory appeal; living a life that is pleasing to her soul. She can see, taste, feel, touch and hear everything that life has to offer, and it manifests through the glow of her skin, the smile on her face, the melodious sound of her voice and the healing in her touch. She's attractive and attracting from within.

Sagacious: *The SWSS Woman* is empathetic yet, perceptive and discerning. She has the ability to see the unseen; to understand difficult ideas, situations and make sound decisions.

Supportive: *The SWSS Woman* nourishes her energy and uses wisdom in expending it. She is aware of when she needs to apply her own oxygen mask to replenish & rejuvenate herself which allows her to give from a place of fullness. She isn't a martyr. She supports others wholeheartedly all the while setting boundaries relying on her inner-G to guide her on when to draw the line.

Stimulating: *The SWSS Woman* ignites others! She is a stimulant for growth and change. She fans the flames of those whose light has dimmed. She is exciting and enlivens those around her. She is a woman of action and it is contagious!

Singleness of Heart: *The SWSS Woman* has a pure heart. She has no hidden agendas or motives. She seeks to deposit positive, impacting truths into everything she takes on. Playing her role in the evolution of greatness is her soul's desire.

WHAT SOUL WEALTH MEANS TO ME

I am the youngest of seven children. Several years ago, I lost three of my sisters to death as the result of illness and addiction. My sisters were not just my sisters they were instrumental in caring for me. Losing them has left a hole in my heart. I've spent the last few years of my life searching for replacements that could fill that void. After five years I had given up and just went about my way all the while longing to connect with women who were ambitious, of integrity and wanted to step into their God given purpose. I connected to my new sisters last year at the 2018 Soul Sun and Spa event sponsored by Soul Wealth. I am honored to be a part of an amazing tribe of phenomenal, powerful and loving women who have become my sisters. Before joining the Soul Wealth community, I was mentally, physically and emotionally broken. Soul Wealth and the relationships I have established have restored my faith, trust and self-worth. Most importantly, Soul Wealth has confirmed that my vision to assist women healing via travel is so needed.

Shay Sane
CEO/Founder, BGTM/BGoTravel
www.blackgirltravelmovement.com

When I say I love this woman, words barely can describe why. Vikki Johnson is authentic, loving, a mentor, someone you can confide in knowing whatever was told to her won't be repeated, a true sister friend. I was drowning and she gently grabbed my hand and said this to me, "welcome to Soul Wealth a sacred sisterhood where you will be healed." Tears running down my face - I thank you so much. I can breathe now. I am no longer drowning. Life is so good.

Janice Carter

Soul Wealth is as the name implies, a means of enriching the essential part of each one of us. As the Bible declares, we became living souls. It also declares that we are better together than we are independently. Nobody has everything, but everybody has something…more often than not, that something can be found within the soul wealth sister-hood. A connected soul is a wealthy soul. THAT is what Soul Wealth means to me!! For this I am grateful.

Dr. Lauretta Halstead

Founder, Contemplative Conversations

Dr. Vikki Johnson in her sweet quiet way came to the table where I was eating with other sisters. They were speaking to her, and of course she talked to them. Then sat across from me. I said hello, and she said hi back. Then she asked me a question: What have I been doing or what will I be doing? Something to that effect. I remember telling her what my experience with men and my healing. Then I began to talk about my business. She looked at me and asked me several questions in her quiet way. I thought I was answering them, but Vikki was getting to a point. My business was more about what I am called to do versus who the business 'be'. In that instance, a new name was born that will hold space for what I have been doing. Vikki Johnson gave me a word from the Lord abouthow my business will flourish, some of the things I am supposed to be doing, and some of the people I am to work with. Then she said, "follow me." I was so excited, but the twinkle in her eyes made me super curious. She gave me a photo shoot that became part of my marketing. My God the vision she saw helped me to see bigger.

During the photo shoot, Vikki said something that made me want to drop to my knees and thank God and kiss her. That morning she was given a gift to give to me, and she honored God (dess). I had no idea when I dreamt of a tree a week or so before I came that I would encounter that tree. After our meet and greet on Thursday, I felt led to go to the labyrinth. I sat on one bench and admired the rock people someone had made of stones. I got up and went to the next bench; as I waited, I heard "go hug the tree". I looked up saw the tree from my dreams in front of me.

I talked to and hugged that tree the entire time I was there. Who knew? But God! My faith has/is being increased.

Tresa Simmons
The Womb Space

Soul Wealth is knowing, understanding and believing that my mere presence on this earth is indicative that I am worthy of living a full life and experiencing full love. Soul Wealth cannot be attained by the collecting of dangling external nuggets that promise quick prosperity.It rejects the call of comparison and the temptation of material attainment. Soul Wealth is a constant return to the essence of the spirit force within. It is a reminder that I am already divinely and richly equipped with all that I need to prosper and thrive. If I speak

the truths that emanate from that core and align my words, actions, deeds authentically I will receive an internal certificate of deposit that will guarantee reward and wealth far above and beyond my initial investment. Soul Wealth is about a spiritual metamorphosis with multilayered revelations of my best self; and I love it.
Dr. Phillis Linnes

Soul Wealth is a currency system among sisters. Each sister comes with the intention of identifying and/or enhancing "her personal value." Collectively, the intrinsic values of each sister help to determine the sisterhood's economic health and hence the well-being of all the women connected via Dr. Vikki Johnson's powerful Soul Wealth movement. It is a movement!
Vivian Smallwood

Dr. Vikki Johnson is a powerful conduit for God via Soul Wealth. I am constantly amazed at how God uses Vikki to connect others, touch the lives of others and inspire by simply BEING. Her words carry weight. She is a mouthpiece for God that results in transformation, inspiration and radiance. Vikki Johnson is the embodiment of SOUL WEALTH!
Anna Debose Hankins
Human Potential Specialist and
Founder of Radiance Woman

I did not know how much abundance was available to me, until Soul Wealth. It introduced me to the currency of sisterhood and that changed everything in my life. In the darkest moments of my life, it has been the Soul Wealth movement that pushed me out of the valley, and back to the top of the mountain. Soul Wealth has shown me that the key to living my best life is living it with disruptive authenticity. Soul Wealth has fortified my faith when I was losing my optimism. Soul Wealth is the part of my life where there is perpetual abundance. This sisterhood is fertile, fruitful and multiplies blessings in my life. Thank you, Dr. Vikki Johnson for your yes! Your unclouded vision helped me see things more clearly.

Thema Azize Serwa
Pioneer and Owner, The Womb Sauna

Soul Wealth means self check - reminding me of the importance of self-care and to give myself permission to pour into myself with the same level of love and compassion in which I pour into others, particularly my patients.

Dr. Pamela Hall

Because of YOU and Soul Wealth, I know what it's like for a sister of prominence to genuinely want me to WIN with no strings or contingencies attached. Soul Wealth to me is operating out of overflow and abundance, instead of scarcity. So much so that you have emotional and spiritual wealth to share with others. Soul Wealth has encouraged me to operate from a place of overflow. Thank you, Dr. Vikki!!!

Dr. Trenace Nikki Richardson

Soul Wealth is cultivated internally with external payoffs. Once you get it and implement it in your daily experience then your life will never be the same.

Denise Hart

Soul Wealth has afforded me with true, authentic, organic opportunities and relationships. I now have relationship equity.
Rosaline "Heavenly Bodies" Law

Soul Wealth is about being FREE to be me without apology!
Xenia Grimes

Soul Wealth has given me moments away from the noise to a place of joy, peace, tranquility, clarity, direction and wealth for my entire being (my soul); at points where change and transition were required to BE a better Leslie. Soul Wealth exposed me to affluent women who embrace one another, encourage one another and teach one another (iron sharpens iron) to be free and the BEST she can be. Soul Wealth is a vision that Dr. Vikki Johnson lives and draws willing women to partake of the fruit and experience. My soul is wealthy because of SOUL WEALTH.
Leslie Atley

Soul Wealth has impacted me in many ways. It challenges me to be bold and beautiful inside and out. It challenges me to focus on self-love. Soul Wealth has connected me to some special, amazing, awesome sisters that have encouraged, supported, taught and just simply embraced me. It has taught me how to just be FREE and to operate from my overflow. My connection to Dr. Vikki Johnson helps me live my life like it is golden.
Jennifer Lanier

I found me through Soul Wealth. Yep! As crazy as that may sound to someone else, Soul Wealth helped me to find my voice and taught me it was OKAY to JUST BE ME UNAPOLOGETICALLY.I learned to reframe my story which helped me to see the value of experiences life has taught me. I learned the importance of relational equity and the sacredness of sisterhood. Because of Soul Wealth, I am living the best days of my life and embracing the GREATNESS of who I am.
Shauntia Wright Stanback

Soul Weal means my ENTIRE life is wealthy. My relational, financial, spiritual, emotional, physical and mental wealth. The Soul Wealth house/community is my first stop resource to everything I need. Soul Wealth has reminded me of the power I have to live the unedited, unapologetic version of myself. It pushes me to dream bigger and gives me the courage to go after my dreams. It heals, sets free and delivers. Most importantly for me, Soul Wealth healed the hurt from past female relationships and gave me relational wealth. Countless times since high school female friends have walked away from me with no regard, leaving me to feel abandoned and unworthy. Little did I know that those patterns would follow me throughout my adulthood causing me not to trust women or let them get too close to me. The few times I let my guard down I was betrayed. The last time that happened, Vikki encouraged me not to allow one bad encounter to stop me from cultivating friendships with other women. Once I allowed God to heal those wounds, my soul was ready for the relational wealth I now have. It's everything to me. What I thought I lost from past relationships; God restored in abundance. Now I'm surrounded by a sisterhood tribe that goes beyond anything I could ever imagine!
Amira F. Scott

SOUL WEALTH has been instrumental in changing the trajectory of my life. I have become a better mother, sister, friend, future wife (smile), author, preacher,entrepreneur, and overall woman. I have obtained a level of freedom that I would have never imagined. SOUL WEALTH has blessed me to be a blessing to others. I can truly be A.T. H.I.S. Service with authenticity, transparency, humility, integrity, and self-awareness.

Sarita Price

What Soul Wealth means to me is mind, body and spirit alignment with the energy of abundance and the willingness to heal any mental or emotional block that opposes our right to experience various forms of prosperity, including matters of the heart. Soul Wealth to me is both an invitation to explore and expand beyond inherited limits.

La Tonia Taylor, ReBirth Int'l
"ReBirth and Emerge Transformed"
http://about.me/LaToniaTaylor

Soul Wealth is being driven directly to the destination where you didn't think you belonged, but you were already destined for. Once you step on the land of your destination, soul wealth is the access and accumulation of prosperity not only financially but in mind, body and spirit. It already belongs to you and no one can take it from you. Soul wealth is your manifestation of greatness and wholeness, your vision and purpose brought to life.

LaQuisha Hall
www.ConfidentCanvas.com

Soul Wealth is an abundance of courage and tenacity that leads to spiritual and emotional health. It gives you the power of endurance to face life's obstacles while gaining strength and fortitude to cultivate spiritual growth. Soul wealth gives you opportunities to use life's experiences to impart wisdom and to positively impact the lives of others. The radiance that soul wealth produces inspires others to want the inner peace and happiness that soul wealth brings.

Dr. Machell Town

Soul Wealth means love, intention, working beyond what's comfortable, but what's needed. It is all that we are and all that we aren't. Vikki develops women from the inside out, challenging, testing, moving and creating the person we all strive to become. Once you meet Vikki, you immediately claim her as your BEST FRIEND! I leave you with this thought: "being wealthy is an internal state of mind. I AM South Wealth!"

Falisa Tittle

What does Soul Wealth mean to me? I can't explain it in a sentence; but these words capture my thoughts: disruptor, abundance, massive, faith, overflowing, multitude, connections, authentic and purpose.

Neddra King
Expert Travel Advisor
Elite Travel by Neddra

Not to sound cliché, but Soul Wealth is genuinely beyond description. What I can say however, is that my experience with this mastermind collective of sisterhood has added to my life beyond measure. From personal mentoring with Dr. Vikki, to seeing the behind the scenes success of people on journeys like mine! The accountability, inspira-tion and motivation never stop; and so, to me... Soul Wealth means FORWARD! It's a hidden treasure, with a fly fearless leader, and I'm really blessed to be a part.

Avery "Lady A" Atkinson
www.ladyaglobal.com
Passport Life, Founder

Soul Wealth means Sisters coming together:
Supporting
Openhearted
Unanimously
Learning with understanding from

Well
Educated
Able
Loving
Talented
Heroines showing us how to make IT HAPPEN NOW for
ourselves!The Lady
Paula Frazier

....because the Soul is the seat of our emotions, Soul Wealth, to me, means being healthy emotionally as well as spiritually. Emotions can be described as energy-in-motion and therefore, Soul Wealth also reminds me of the importance of managing the energetic resonance that I project to myself first and then to the world. Soul Wealth is an all-encompassing, life changing way of being.

Dr. M. Yewong

Soul Wealth is a powerful, motivating and spiritual support of sisterhood. Soul Wealth has allowed me to overcome fears, awaken my soul and brought me into an abundance of joy, peace and everyday happiness within myself.

Catrina Stroman

Soul Wealth is the pristine air I now breathe, as it is God's untainted representation of himself, manifested through Dr. Vikki that consis-tently speaks to who I AM and who I am called to BE authentically ME. It has exposed me to a plethora of spiritual, natural, and business opportunities and has encouraged me to pursue greatness in thought and deed, first personally, with my tribe, my sphere of influence and beyond. I so greatly embrace the network, movement and vision of Soul Wealth as it has also given me a portal to experience LIFE at an-other dimension, be more purposeful, and live life with great expecta-tions of my temporal and eternal future.Love you Dr. Vikki Johnson!

Portia S. Wheatley

a.k.a.Widowed Diva

Order your copies at www.vikkijohnson.com

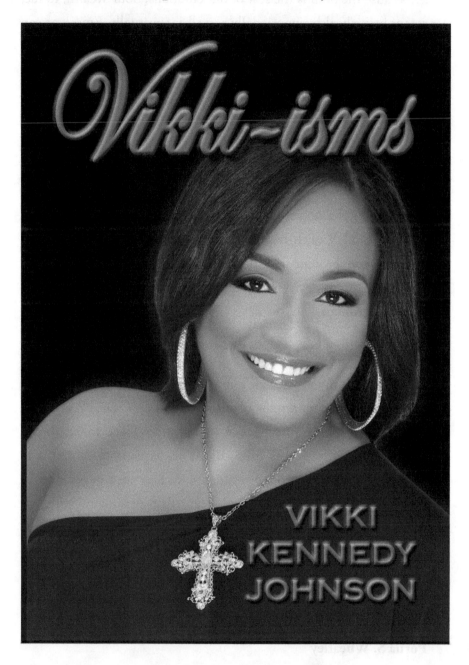

Order your copies at www.vikkijohnson.com

CPSIA information can be obtained
at www.ICGtesting.com
Printed in the USA
FSHW010750041119